CISTERN LATITUDES

Poems by
James Duncan

ROADSIDE PRESS

For Amelia

Table of Contents

Strays..1

Conjoined 2

Homecoming...3

Transference 4

September...5

Umbra 6

Windfall..7

Saturnalia 8

Downtown..9

Vulpes 10

Somnambulist 11

Tulip 12

Gossamer 13

Celestial 14

Resurrection 15

Tourist.. 17

Familiars... 18

Prophecy 19

Storm King 20

Nuclear Shadow... 21

Remainders 22

Affliction 23

Bestowal 24

Immanence 25

Emissary 26

A Boy Named Ropinan.. 28

Legacy... 29

Marathon 31

All You Can Carry 32

Entropy 33

Barbarous.. 34

Ordination.. 36

Abyssal 37

Pastoral 38

Migration 39

Pioneer 40

Wane 41

Illumine 42

Dusk 44

Solace 45

Pemaquid 46

Declarations 47

Canoe 48

Sawdust 49

An Unordered List of Things That Remain 50

Entwined 52

Fugue 53

Recriminations 54

Parables 55

Bereave 57

Acre 58

Stage Right 59

Dandelions in the Dark 60

Fedora 61

Tao of the City 62

Orchid 64

Great Plains and Galaxies Beyond 66

Demarcation 67

Intimations 68

Intercontinental 69

Grunewald 70

Publication Notes 72

About the Author 73

Cistern Latitudes (noun): small descents into spaces and moments that once witnessed tectonic shifts in destiny that are now as silent and still as subterranean pools of water, clear and dark and carrying the truth that life and the world may have lost its way, that tragedy may linger in the corners of our past, but there are still latitudes and geographies out there that harbor safe, calm, and magical futures if we look for them.

Strays

Lynette took my hand and led me behind the gas station and into the woods until she stopped and said *this is where my sister and I would hide from our mother for days at a time, where we lived alone and fed off gas station junk food, afraid, aggrieved, hounded by sunsets and strays…*

then she'd stare into the middle distance, lost to some other time but not to some other place—it was this place here, now, forever haunted by things no child should experience until we walked back to the car to find a dark bar to drink and speak of other things as the southern California sun raged with fevered despair, weeping at its useless might until one day it too might fall into the roiling emerald-gray Pacific to meet the Great Mother of us all

Conjoined

there you are, there you were
a ghost among the dacite rocks

lining the coast of Pacific Grove
where Steinbeck once scrounged

for crab and mollusk, clam and fish
to feed his starving wife and self

a ghost among the many, alone
among the stones, how many of

us stand there now and stare out
to sea? out to the waves beckoning

us to join them? are you there now?
am I? alone as the waves overlap?

ghosts conjoined by time and place,
the dacite rocks, igneous volcanic

as you were, as you forever are

Homecoming

slip between the old wooden rowboats down into the water, listen to them bump one another as the tide comes in, the depths swirling beneath, the boathouse decrepit now, its secrets gone, its beams and supports rotting, creaking under the weight of nostalgia, those wedding party guests as dried and dull as the maple leaves caught in cobwebs in the corners, the sunlight fighting its way in through a decayed roof, the water lapping, whispers fictionalized and cinematic as you bob under the wooden planks down in the dark and remember how you both removed your hearts and placed them into the water, letting them drift out into the lake, beyond tropics Capricorn and Cancer, through the many seas and oceans where storms rage and loves fade, grow hazy with time, lost like ships that never return to port, the eternal possibility, the waiting, the constriction of lungs holding air down beneath the places where rowboats once bobbed, tied to piers, waiting for someone to come make use of them, give them purpose, but they too are gone, just dark swirling water in their place, a few bubbles, gentle tides, and a single red leaf tumbling in the breeze coming through the open boathouse doors, dropping in the lifeless water below.

Transference

just because you're gone doesn't mean this place
is finished with you, the dust motes in the sunlight
ebb and float around your shape, the love you held
in your heart as kinetic as ever, your soul resting in
inverse to time, to space, to the stillness of this room
without you

September

cusp of autumn evening dim and up into the attic where boxes and crates have waited for 10, 15 years or more covered in dust and silent heartache // leaves now pepper the lawn, yellow and red and lonesome brown as up here there's middle school love gone wrong in old journals, names of girls now women with families and names of teachers now retired, or worse, and beneath the journals are envelopes of love letters on paper thin and crinkled as the wind ebbing gently through the trees outside the small attic windows, the cool air seeping through slats and broken glass \\ there's a place where sunsets never quite go away and dawn doesn't come, a place on ruled paper, history scrawled in pencil in cursive, swirling eagerness for future destinies dreamed about in homerooms and on bus rides home, journals and papers boxed away as journeys began, never knowing all that waited beyond the sunset fire // and now, knowing, feeling it all like slivers working under skin, I fold the paper away and close the lid, descend to the lawn for cool comfort, erasure calm, merciful nights to help put those old futures behind me and a new past somewhere ahead

Umbra

a basement space in the dark of the soul where little specs of dust fall from the wood beams as someone above walks restless, waiting, near panic, not knowing there are those below who listen, who feel this unending agony that nothing will shine a light down through those wooden slats into the depths, into the cistern latitudes where anxiety seethes and grows and one day rises like the scent of wet earth into the world like a specter of blue silent Friday nights come back for vengeance but finding the house empty all this time, the sounds and dust and wood just an illusion all this time, a choking and somber indelicate truth that time means nothing to no one no more

Windfall

sour scent of old apples in the sun,
tart and lush and warm, the tufts
of grass rising thick from the earth
at the base of the fruit trees lining
the path to the old farmstead, the
dog running ahead, the sun falling
behind, the windows watch as you
approach, staring hollow and weary,
remembering your footfalls, recalling
the somnolent evenings together, but
someone has left the door ajar here,
the wilderness and farmstead one
lonely embrace of vines and timber,
and soon the wind will take down all
the foundations this lonesome world
has ever known or will ever know,
as the grass grows lush in the silence
and the dog runs circles in the sunset

Saturnalia

they tell you to leave the wine in the kitchen and partake
of respite conversations in the sun, middle-aged managers
and painters and even a regular on NPR, augural festivities
of what might be if you honed and hardened your soul's
anticipation into diamond-point tedium, rung after rung,
you see the ages unfolding into sons and daughters too
young to drink but sipping aperol spritzers espousing their
college-entry wisdom as a neighbor's nephew's band begins
in the backyard near the gazebo, the in-ground pool in the
background, five young men playing Grateful Dead songs
for happy accountants with ponytails, upward mobile wives
who commute two hours three days a week to manage text-
book developers, big money in the right circles, and now
they're playing Phish and the sun cascades with anguish
because you can't, you just can't see how you'd fill a house
this size with anything more than regret, sectional couches
spilling infallible warnings as you go back through to the
kitchen, take your unopened bottle of ten-dollar wine, leave
your body behind to mimic the final months of this charade,
and there you go out into the sidewalk of small town subur-
bia to find the fire that will end this chapter and write the
next one in ash against clear blue skies a dozen states and
rivers and lifetimes to the west

Downtown

something between sleet and snow cuts sideways across the portion of downtown street that he can see through the pizzeria window and the sitting area where a family eats from red plastic trays of cheese and pepperoni slices, and a middle-aged man reading by the front window for an hour now, slowly working on the last bite or two of sausage and onion though he doesn't seem to be ready to leave anytime soon

he couldn't see how anyone just sits there in a pizzeria with a book like that alone, just eating in silence without any TV or radio or someone to talk to like Salvi in the back or Bonilla out for deliveries, either one of them always talking while they ate, stories of baseball or boxing or what their kids did last week, and to sit there and read alone for so long didn't make sense, but the pizzas didn't stop just because the snow fell in flickering droves illuminated by street lights and the yellow neon slice of pizza in the window, bright in such stark contrast to the customers in the dim eating area, soft conversations, ceiling fan meditations, all while he pounded the next ball of dough flat, spinning it, pushing out the edges to hold the sauce and cheese in the middle, finally slipping it into the oven, a quick basic pie for the next winter stragglers who'd come in and sit in the spaces now vacated by the family and the man who sat reading for almost an hour, all gone, leaving him alone with the radio set to the Patriots game, Salvi in the back making stromboli, tomorrow's sauce, a long night ahead with nothing else to do but watch something between sleet and snow cut sideways across the downtown street beyond the window alone, alone, alone

Vulpes

silver foxtail breath running into winter skies fraught with
roil, starless, cloudful, impending ice storms with pellet cru-
elties that peck away at whatever comforts we've accrued to
shield ourselves from such ever-present misfortune, inevita-
ble

hooded figures hustle down State Street, discarded Christ-
mas trees in inchoate dreams, silent envelopment as the
sudden snow formulates into view and amasses in thin
choirs along curbs, between cobbles, shoulders of children
and parents hurrying inside with groceries, backpacks, shov-
els at the ready to forge hope out of crystalline ballast pow-
dered across the cityscape lamppost night

watching from the second story bedroom window, curtains
drawn closed, baseboards ticking their thermal poetry, we
descend into sheets together, comforters, feather down
duvets in clean hues of pink to shiver cool our bare skin with
rhubarb lamplight slipping in to meet us, filtered through
closed eyes, down into our den where hearts and lungs pulse
vulpes wild through the night holding us tight to arctic
assurances and the hope for warmer seasons beyond

Somnambulist

you say you don't hear
me get out of bed ten times a night
when the medications
grip me with claws and demands
but I keep thinking
the bedroom door creaking will wake
you, or the bathroom fan,
the groan of the hallway floor in that one
spot that sounds like it
could give in and collapse at any moment

it never does, and you never fully wake,
only adjust and burrow
against me as I slip into bed to try for another
hour or two of sleep,
and how your warm lips find mine in the dark
is a wonderment I'll always
seek no matter how late or how early or how many
times I wake at night, alone

but never really alone
these days

Tulip

the red tulip
waits
on the table
an eyelash of the gods
a remnant of what was
now
wilting, fading
holding
on without water or
sleep

in the sun

Gossamer

how fleeting these images, still-frame transparencies tethered to another existential plane // moving images moored to a groove in the brain leading to a realm only passable in the deepest ravines of REM sleep \\ delicate adventures that tendril back to yesterday, back years into other dreams that traversed these same canyons and city streets, these same fields of wheat and dilapidated homes on the edge of a prairie, the same neighborhoods and hotels, a place as real as any other, as fleeting as any other

oh, you think this existence here as you read this is forever compared to the ephemeral films of nocturnal revelry? the silk and chiffon fog that separates the two, the dozen, the infinite may seem as frail as your breath curling silver in the cold morning air, but it's as real as any other elemental actuality // the filaments that connect all these worlds into one great life—so very long and yet over already—sparkle in the morning dew and hold delicate the possibilities unachievable on this side of the plane, where time clocks are punched, where boots march on bones, where flags snap in the wind to celebrate weak and terrible men, but once you slipstream into the gossamer curtains of revelation, behold—

you will know no boundaries one day, embraced by sunsets warm and welcoming as you disappear into diaphanous horizons with one final strand that will loosen its hold on the now and cast you into the next

Celestial

homeless mothers and college kids
   and those drum circle panhandlers
with the dogs all standing beneath the
   train bridge in downtown Northampton,
a sudden torrential deluge of rain, waiting
   together for a break in the onslaught that
came out of nowhere, the sound like static
   on an old television set against the small
dog's bark, the drummer's laughter, the
   college girls from Smith gasping as rain
slips through girders onto fresh summer skin,
   no one really speaking to each other, just
huddled in tight formations, watching the
   neon shimmer across the liquified blacktop
as the 8:10 Express to Springfield passes
   overhead, blotting out all sound, even the
rotation of the Earth in stereo—and all at once,
   it stops // everything falls to nuclear implosion
'til the drums start, the girls all begin walking,
   dogs bark, cars honk at the next stop light,
a man with a Santa beard asks for change,
   church bells and Wall Street and battleships,
the dissipation of light and sound and matter
   in all directions as rain sweeps toward gutters
and the clouds roll over in their celestial beds
   to dream of sea change and supplication
whispered to the gussets of fate between each
   one of us tonight and tomorrow and forever more

Resurrection

from a window overlooking downtown, maybe that intersection with the bank and the bar and the theater // maybe the top floor of the hotel where you can see all the way down Broadway to the railroad trellis // maybe it was called the Gideon, the Plaza Azteca, the Wilshire // maybe it never had a name, not after the gutting began // maybe the carpet pulled up revealed hidden money, passports, notes of desperation // maybe they found rusted razors in the walls behind the porcelain sinks // maybe the echoes of passion remained in each room // maybe violence // maybe the soft sobs of the lonely // maybe the ballroom still has the old piano // maybe it plays at midnight, just a few keys, just when no one else is around // maybe the staff knew about that // maybe they didn't // maybe the celebrity chef who filmed an episode of his TV show in the kitchen still thinks about the beautiful wallpaper that is no longer there // or maybe it is still there, so long as the chef can remember the textured ivy pattern // maybe there are still people in those gutted rooms celebrating New Year's Eve // maybe a birthday // maybe a summer getaway // maybe the decision to finally end things // maybe a last call on the phone to beg forgiveness, make things work at last // maybe there are no ghosts // maybe we're all still there in those rooms, those halls, those elevators, where now only the cables swing in the dark // or maybe from the window overlooking downtown, as the theater lets out patrons on their way to cocktail bars and cafes and safe warm beds at home, there is a single soul left to stare out at the lights of this town, a town in any state, any valley // maybe it whispers a name // or maybe it is

content to wait for whatever future comes next for the old
hotel // content with its choices, its solitude, its perch above
the lights and the darkness and the world that never stops
just a moment to look up and see nothing at all

Tourist

in the silence of the church I think of our trip to Plymouth
Rock one November, touring another silent church and
signing the guest book and marveling that Mick Jagger,
Elton John, and David Bowie had all toured the church that
day until you told me, in my youthful ignorance, that anyone
can sign any name into the book and it was just a prank, and
how red and warm my face became with my mistake, how
the church smelled of dust and candles and earth carried in
by the shoes of tourists, the wooden structure groaning in
the coastal winds, and now I sit here, churches and states
and lost lifetimes away and watch as a line of well wishes
sends you into the next world, and I stand, walk to the guest
book in the hall, and sign a name for you, one more tourist
in this world trying to smile, but failing

Familiars

a collective of moonlight pulses beating Morse code commands through the evening // you send these curious agents into the sky, down streets and highways, out to fetch milk and eggs, a newspaper, a match, a rabbit's foot, eye of newt, or perhaps a bottle of red or white or anything in between // they return, bringing stories and sorrow, ghosts trailing after them like the red taillights of an endless traffic jam spanning the horizon, reminding you of night drives up the 101 in California or I-35 outside Austin, I-87 up the Hudson River valley on a Friday night, memories building miles, seeking collaborators, allies, new horrors on the wing, sweeping the moonlit sky, searching through galaxies and heavenly bodies, each ache and pain doing your bidding, taking you deeper, further, higher, and someday out of reach of all these human directives, far into the rushing bloodstream of the insular moon above, who watches, but does not yet speak

Prophecy

a guardrail bent and demented,
twisting into darkness as we pass

some bad omen of humanity's fate
a car crash we won't see coming

and whoever comes next will understand
as little as we do now, passing in the night

Storm King

the road will jackknife in the dark, twist through crags of stone and forests of red-gold leaves tumbling in the October wind, wind whispering the names of witches hung and burned in Colonial days of yore, cruel ministrations from puritan faiths now disguised as modern rural civility, the doors shut and windows drawn as you pass through the monied hideaway villages along the Hudson // the road plunges you into dark tunnels and gloomy hollows until the bridge spans the Hudson, opens the skies, and brings you into the bustling highways that scream for you to forget the past, blare fictions into your throat as speeds untenable, and off you go on a straightaway home—but don't you dare forget that those twisting jackknife roads in the hills and breakneck ridges along the river remain, their secrets intact, their mysteries seeping ever outward, calling from lonely cliffs, hugging the waters of the flowing Hudson, ready to pull this world back into the primordial haze of myth and legend, of whispers unanswered in the crags of stone and forests of red-gold leaves tumbling in the October wind

Nuclear Shadow

ice cubes sit atop the soil
slowly melting, feeding the
weeping fig, a lone survivor
of seven moves in six years,
subways and box trucks and
the trunk of an old Honda,
poverties and bouts of madness,
broken luck and idle sadness,
and now the plant waits
idle and still in a corner like
a nuclear shadow, leftover
from a blinding explosion,
as one lifetime ends—one
begins elsewhere, the pages
of the calendar flipping and
falling away while the plant
lives on, shedding leaves like
brown beetles, little piles of
what was, replaced by green
hopes of what might be, the
same, the same, but nothing
will ever look or feel the same,
just quiet, still, sitting beside
a potted weeping fig in new
corners in new cities, fed by
ice cubes sitting atop the soil

Remainders

stone stairs rise from a trickling fountain into the pine forest halfway up a mountain in Vermont / take them up one by one to a moss-covered statue of a wood nymph where you can stop / turn around \ and look down on rolling hills: through the trees a distant apple orchard, the small town of Bennington, and there before you at the bottom of the long line of steps covered in autumn detritus is the stone mansion, the heart of your old college now closed // abandoned \\ a castle of New England elitism, though you felt nothing of the sort during your time there: poor and working as a night janitor while sitting in cold classrooms as the ancient radiators clanked and hissed, discussing Gothic literature and chemical compounds, mathematics and remainders, Shakespeare and Mise en Scène, planned an engagement and wandered the cathartic wilderness of love \ and then, when the school released you to the world: aimless and alone, a long trail of debt, medical bills, lonely one-room apartments, midnights huddled at empty windows wondering if dawn should even bother—but it did, indifferent to human plight, patterns holding despite torment or joy \ and it led you again to those stone steps to look down upon snowflakes falling through the trees, gentle and buoyant \\ like the wood nymph beside you posing mid-dance in marble, you remain, and will even after the universe falls in a hail of stars—you will remain.

Affliction

with no subtle pageantry the small rodents of the natural
world descend from the trees to devour green chestnuts on
the front steps, cascading detritus and chewed husk in all
directions, delighted consumption, basking bright in the
summer sun as within I wither away in shadow, looking
upon the world through a window shade of blue, replete
with disease, my slow recovery in solitude amongst books
in neat piles, fastidious organization and humming fans bil-
lowing my sick room as I wait and watch the local rodents
celebrate another season without finance or time-cards or
weaponry or nuclear codes or advertising money or corpo-
rate executive officers or the empty rooms in an empty house
where children once played, now ghosts that haunt dreams
and makes one wonder what else waits beyond the veil as
recovery crawls through the veins and cells and daydream
hopes within me, sitting by the window in this summer of
contagion

Bestowal

a carton of fresh eggs waits on the stoop, gifts from unknown
patrons, from unknown animals in small pens who inspect
the world with spastic darting eyes, gods to sinners unrec-
ognized, monsters to creatures infinitesimal, caged in their
pens and waiting for hands to come from the giants in the
hills to abscond with their treasure, their lifeline, their fate,
packaged and sold to those who open doors to empty stoops,
curls of cold exhalations twisting into the wind, wondering
why or how luck found them that day

Immanence

pink glasses and book on the nightstand
a reminder of your temporary absence \\
blue afternoon light a somber embankment
against the tide of my wanting, my waiting

then outside a subtle hint of keys rattle and fit
into a lock // and the world alights with you

Emissary

empty living rooms, empty kitchens
sinks full of plastic dishware, stained curtains
the smell of rubbing alcohol, Lysol, and bleach;
empty bedrooms, empty home offices
filled with binders listing medications and
medical appointments, staffing schedules,
a desk calendar where the house manager
crosses out Chris and writes her own name
crosses out Tabitha and writes her own name
crosses out vacation and writes double shift
her photo with every resident on the wall,
the one in the wheelchair, the one with dementia,
the one with severe autism, the one who just died,
all of them smiling when they're with her,

I wonder when she has time for her family, the kids
in the photos stuck half beneath the desk calendar;
I am there to fix the dryer, vacuum it out so it
doesn't set the house on fire, check the fire escapes
in each of the six bedrooms, check the smoke
detectors, the extinguishers, the annual check-up,
wandering room to room, group home to group
home when everyone is away, a silent patrol
for people who don't know I exist, for people who don't
exist themselves outside of a group home, outside
of the public's eye or ability to care, outside of
some overworked house manager's heart, hidden
from a world of TikTok dances and angry patriotism,
relegated to quiet rooms in quiet houses haunted

by the man who sometimes fixes their dishwasher
and then slips out the back door to a world just as solitary,
empty kitchen, empty bedroom, empty home

A Boy Named Ropinan

fields of patchwork honeysuckle beside a school, beside a treeline hiding a steep slope to a ravine where he fell thirty years ago, a boy who called himself Ropinan, a self-given nickname he used when mimicking an ape, a Kong-like creature, beating his chest but just a boy, round and soft, eager for friends or any attention at all in the long Bataan Death March we called middle school where bullies and friends blend into a mirage of impermanence that might cause a young boy to make a fool of himself, to summersault with Chris Farley energy across a field of honeysuckle and fall through the treeline, down a ravine, injuring himself to the point of requiring rescue—and that's where my memories of Ropinan end, nothing more, no images or snapshots, no beating the chest or cafeteria conversation, he is simply gone from history, nothing but a field mowed down to hard brown stubble beside an empty school thirty years later, a summer without birdsong, a boy lost to time.

Legacy

February are inconsolable—
my final surviving grandmother
passed away that month, and
for much of my life she would sit on
the end of her long brown couch
and expect a kiss and an "I love you"
the moment I walked in the door,
certainly before we raided her pantry,
as hungry grandkids are known to do,
and I was happy to do it (tell her I loved
her, I mean, and raid the pantry, I suppose)
she let me eat Planters Cheez Balls after
school and made the best potato salad,
the best meatballs, the best homemade
Thousand Island dressing for the best
fresh garden salads in the summertime //
she taught me about empathy and
about kindness, not to hit my sister or anyone
for that matter // we protect each other,
not hurt each other \\ and when I was a little
boy, maybe four or five, I had a lot of
stomach issues, going to the bathroom was
a struggle, but she would come in and sing me
songs and it made me feel better, and
if I was embarrassed about it
she would sit outside the door and do it
without question, for as long as I needed
but by the end she was repeating herself all
the time and didn't always know who

we were, talked to people who weren't there,
people who had died years before,
siblings, parents, friends, telling her it was
her time, she said, and then she left,
but we still own her Bible, and her brown
couch is still somewhere, some other hand-me-down
home, and her kindness is within me, within
my sister, and that is a finer thing than a thousand
marble headstones or holy temples, the passing
down of goodness from one age to the next,
the only kind of legacy that matters

Marathon

you end the phone call with the doctor and look around the empty room // no one reaches for the harrowing baton that is now forming a sinkhole within you // the length of a shadow across the hardwood floor as evening twilight darkens is a companion of sorts, though a silent one, distant, evaporated, extinct, you weep // then stop, rise and go out, merge into the streets of this upstate city to be near moving celestials racing past you on the sidewalk, fleeing through rain and neon and when you run out of hours and energy and hope you return to the floor in the dark and measure it all again // the length of a shadow, the shape of a dream, the gray sense of lives divided by feet of dirt, shovel after shovel like the ticking second hand on an infinite clock somewhere out there in the dark // you weep, then stop // you keep moving forward no matter what

baton in hand

All You Can Carry

he doesn't see me, he sees a figure, a shape,
and he takes an awkward step or two before
he realizes it's me, doddering closer,
holding himself against my chest as I kneel
before him // his breathing, his panting,
collar loose, his hair becoming my hair, clinging to my clothes
and face \\ time wanes against us both \ I know
this will not happen again and again and again,
only again and that's it \ and when it's over,
the steps in front of the empty house will groan
when I arrive, but only just for me \ I will stand idle
and alone in the cold October wind
as if all that came before was a shapeless void
that I cannot bear to carry
  // but I will

Entropy

the flakes and shards of paint and wood
　fray from this patio decades old, once
new and brown to match the line of old
　trailers nearby, our entropic youth hardly
contained as we imagined ourselves as
　ancient mariners lost at sea, searching for
rhyme and meaning to small lives not
　yet formed into desolate creations marred
by the hells of adulthood, and now here
　the wood rots where you once stood, the
crickets chirp where I once cried out for land
　for lost redeemers to find us, haul us into
the next world so we may dissolve our youthful
　partnership into that of frayed and distant
ghosts who once were and will never be again

Barbarous

the shining glint of the sun
reflecting off the green seas
as you leap from one bed to
the next with your brother
and sister, waving plastic
swords, pillowcase sails
snapping in the wind, eye-
patch heroics, the cries of
triumph and tragedy echo
across infinite waves of yore

while outside the window
seamless birds sing through late-winter air

little scars throbbing

a trove of memories the color of sunlight,
of gold, of teeth set against a hellscape
of aging and death, of teeth set in a smile,
determined to fight through timecards and
gas bills, political vitriol and highway death,
don't think about it, don't peer through the
spyglass into the future, set a different course
across the barbarous seas to innocence and
keep that steady course, if you can

none of us can

no matter how much your rapturous crew

attempts to hold on to those good spirits,
the seas will churn, the ships will falter,
the seamless birds will throb into the far
flung horizon, little scars unending that
no eyepatch or pegleg or chest of silver
will overcome, leaving behind empty beds,
empty rooms, empty hearts that yearn
to raise the sails and cast away from all this
away and away for good and for ever

Ordination

birthday snow, damp and blue
all pockmarked by the feet
of squirrels and rabbits who
roam free throughout Pine Hills

Tuesday morning with no work, no calls,
the phone discarded amongst bedsheet
waves and mountain peaks, the idle
blue hours of waking so very slow

the patter of rain and ice melt on windows
and sidewalks outside, a day and world
getting on with it, no matter the celebrations
here in cold quiet isolation, contemplation

soon enough the axis will tilt and spin
this amalgam of stone and water into
new trajectories, with or without me,
as my bones rest beneath snow and sun

as they do here for just a few minutes more,
casual incineration while thinking about
turning six years old in '86—and I rise, 43
rotations deep, and begin the begin again

the best years of our lives, here and now

Abyssal

crouched on precipice bedrock as waves swell and dash unrelenting against drowned coastlines slipping into the beckoning sea, the lighthouse towering above as you follow primordial sensations, crawling closer to the edge, picking up stones, piling them atop one another in wayward cairns to see who can build one taller than the other, staring out into the deep blue tumult sensing the kinetic concentration of depth and might in the air in the stone in the sea in the earth so far below, the rising swell of the universe destined to meet you at the shore in one great thunderclap at last

for a moment you consider diving headlong into that surging dislocation as gulls cry wild far above in the bright Atlantic sun

yet you remain in intractable defiance // or stoic regret // you have not decided yet

Pastoral

sit behind the final row of homes at the furthest edge of
town, the expanse of tall grass swaying pale in the moon-
light, lightning bugs galaxial sparkling by the thousands
all the way out to the opaque treeline, the distant fringe
of Other, ethereal and eternal, a barrier that also beckons
somehow, coy in meaning and intention like a watchful dog
that may yet bite // dark and impenetrable / monastic // the
jagged pine tree teeth of the world open and swallowing all
the moonlight it can gather while here the lights of human-
ity blink out down the line of homes, the kitchen windows
yellow and sharp, televisions glowing pale blue, little porch
lights, little solar walkways into gardens, out, out, out they
go, leaving only the lightning bugs, the moon, a single dog
barking in the distance until it too gives way to the orchestral
movements of the wind in the distant branches, tall grass
crickets, a feeling of dire isolation at the edge of all things,
crossroads of civilizations // it will pass, all this—the trees
and the homes and the television signals, it will pass // it's
the feeling of this place that will remain after our bones glow
white in the moonlight and the wind curls and instruments
through stone and rock and calls a name no one will hear //
after all else is gone, this will remain

Migration

inert calculations in black and white
dialect through the wires and LEDs
as the crowd of us shuffle from one
meeting to the next, pushing deadlines
and landing planes, circling back, ad-hoc
insinuations and timecards, PTO, MIA

as the rivulets of rain travail the
floor-to-ceiling windows—a map
of the world's aorta migrating out
through the miles and eons, into the
cool calm mineral depths below,
immune to insults or schedules,
simply circulating heedless existence

on the Teams call in a conference room
with eight other silent souls I listen to
a disembodied voice discuss analytics
as I watch the pines in the distant treeline
sway with unfelt wind, clouds curling gray
beyond with geese in a V heading south

I feel my heart beating and listen as
the world goes silent: someone looks
my way, summoned, awaiting my reply

I watch the V of geese pass out of sight

and begin to speak

Pioneer

antecedent legends and points on maps folded by hands
unknown small creases in history, moments unspoken
when it all went south or sometimes west to warmer
climes, east to precursor enlightenment, but we whisper
away north, stars unfading, guiding with assurance that this
world knows more than any human heart about the beating
rhythms of the universe, and if you're true and quiet —
elucidation

Wane

the moon succumbs to wounded skies
sinks into the teeth of this world
into the jagged evergreen treeline

drowning in silent lore

the canoe eases back to shore
insects dancing on the surface of the lake
apocalyptic fires dotting the horizon

a loon calls out—a banishment

this world is not long for any of us;
when we depart, a peaceful silence will come
and run desolation-wild forever

Illumine

at the edge of a lake in the moonlight
majestic with little flickers of white
along the ridges and grooves of the
lapping water—a small lamp appears
in the distant curve of lakeside forest;
a hand-held lamp, oil or otherwise, it
hovers and hues the saplings and pine
trees with golden amber illumination,
something so warm and so small that
steadily edges closer, a firefly in slow-
motion, stopping, waiting at the shore

we stand together, wraiths in the night
separated by earth, water, wind, fire,
elemental disconnection, but tied by
wonderment and curiosity—who else
dares these forests by night, and alone?

the light moves again, and so do I, one
cautious step at a time among stones
and branches washed up on shore, mud
and pools of water heavy with reeds and
cattail swaying in the darkness, my hands
reaching out as the distant light fades
along the shore, reappears, over and
over as we draw near, the wind coiling
across the water of the lake as if to hurry
this meeting in the might, this revelation,
the light blooming, intention burning,

trees and cattails huddling close as I stop
and wait, eyes wide to phosphoresce the
purpose of this shared journey in the dark
as the small bowl of light comes closer
closer yet, even still

Dusk

down the dirt path embankment to the river basin, the per-
fectly rounded stones made smooth by ancient tides rising
and falling before the first mammal took their first breath,
the dam up the river steady with static as tonnage pours over
the weir, fish leaping in the blue hour dusk, memories of
when you drove me all the way down from the Adirondacks
so I could go home, finished with the lonesome wilds, aching
with loss from one funeral after another, wondering if my
own life was worth exploring, you drove me from that tent
and those miseries and brought me home, but you stopped
first, wanting to fish the waters of the Hudson for just a
minute or two, and as you cast your pole I sat on a rounded
stone and closed my eyes, listening to the river, the sound
of my sister reeling in the empty hook, casting again into
that static sound of the waterfall dam, opening my eyes to
an empty embankment years and lifetimes later, our time
ageless as the stars and finite as the casting of your pole,
reeling the line, setting the hook into the lead to stow the
rod and ascend into another lifetime as blue hour dusk fades
to midnight, dawn a distant dream we may never know, but
can hope for; there's always that

Solace

beyond the enclosed back-porch windows
there is a lawn of tall grass and butterflies,
a garden, a Maine skyline rolling blue with
rain on the horizon—not here yet, maybe
never here at all, the greenhouse reflective,
open to a summer heat so thick upon us we
melt with unspoken ease, unworried about
what day of the week it may or may not be

there are some pieces of the universe that
stay the same and no hell or human cruelty
can touch them, they are a wonderment all
their own—and, she says, there's iced tea
brewing and on the way, with a bowl of red
grapes, cheese, crackers—their dog sighs
half asleep on the floor, lost in time, lost in
dreams, unworried about what day of the
week it may or may not be, as it should be

Pemaquid

tendrils of sedition cannot reach us here
the news doesn't appear on smart phones
there is no social media and never was
there are no marches and no boots or knees
      pressing down
on necks in this place where the
sea meets the shore, stones as big as houses along
the coastline, the wind, the gulls

incessant doomscrolling, synapses firing deep
into the night as one app opens, closes, reopens,
searching for the next post, the next hit, micro-
dosing dopamine for no gain or pleasure, only
tired mornings
jagged dreams, unable to stop feeding
on whatever social media might offer next, deep
synaptic fireworks, doomscrolling the night away

but those curling tentacles cannot find us now
we came here hounded by the end of all things
to find the nights long, the sheets cool in the
      ocean breeze
        smelling pine and meadow weeds, wildflowers
in the night, you beside me and me beside you
as we breathe in tune with the heedless waves
slipping along the coastal stones, crawling toward
primordium
      to start again and find
another way home

Declarations

a knife gouged a letter into the white paint and
oak flesh of the bench overlooking the Atlantic ocean

and then it gouged another, a heart,
the staccato imitation of an arrow

plunging through, and two more
letters, forming a declaration of love

only one human, possibly two, knows about
as below the cliff, below the hill of saltgrass swaying

in the wind, the gulls cry out for companionship
and vengeance, and hunger

and the kind of love no human
will ever know

Canoe

oar and paddle into the wrinkled mirror skin of the lake, salmon-pink skies overhead reaching past infinity for neon and magic, the loon calling lonesome as the sun fades to blue and purple and black, the primordial wheel of celestial myth giving way to campfire stories, footsteps in the dark, waters lapping as children nestle into sleeping bags and I sit and stare at empty chairs, worrying about what lies in wait over the next horizon, what fevers we have created to mire the goodness of this world, but whatever apocalyptic inauspicions hide out there, there are still hours of respite in this place, this aching wonderment of earth and moss and water, the canoe that carried us here upside down on the shore, empty chairs by the fire and one last light in my tent calling me to absolve myself of these fears and give my mind over to the other life, and I do

Sawdust

a stool waits in a barn beside a table of rusting tools and sawdust, wood chips and the smell of animals lingering in the dirt floor, the horses and sheep who once resided there before the woodshop became a respite for a man you loved but once stood up to say he'd be right back, and never returned \\ and there you wait, the wind gently pushing at the open barn door, the light shifting in the afternoon hours, and the stool, the sawdust, the kinetic nothingness of loss

An Unordered List of Things That Remain

1. two egg shells broken
in half on a paper towel
in the morning light

2. an empty water dish
on the floor, stained
with age-old saturation

3. the space in the air
where the sound of nails
on hard wood once rattled
through the breeze made
by open window summertime

4. a phantom peripheral
pulling me left to glance
at an unoccupied square
of carpet where dust motes
now dance

5. a feeling of recognition
that a certain feeling
no longer exists

6. two disjointed jungle animals
with broken squeekers and
torn ears, legs flopping and cotton
innards wisp out of gnawed
seams like dead dandelions
ready to take flight

7. a box with a name engraved,
ready

8. a list of things to do but not
the will to do them

9. a window through which no
one looks until the Thursday
garbage pickup has passed so
we don't see all that once remained:
dog bed, collar, leash, etc.

10. and you,
the bluebirds still call out your radiance
in the sunlight

that remains as well

Entwined

I lost you for a moment there, wires and cables and tubes netting you down to that emergency room bed where you stared up at us, unable to speak or remember your name, temporal synaptic idiosyncrasies violating your sense of self and severing the many possible timelines ahead of you as *The Equalizer* played silently on a TV overhead and the halls filled with the moans of the ignored and wounded people of Albany, but now all these weeks later that emergency room where the nurse said he'd seen piss and vomit and death holds someone else's fear and anguish in cupped hands as it held mine, as it held ours, but we are gone—we escaped, survived, held together by hope and desperation that one of those better timelines of yours and mine waits for us at dawn, and we'll follow it together no matter what else it may bring

Fugue

what is lost is found again
    and again
in the blighted ravines of the midnight memory,
headlights streaming over high desert horizons,
    two beams into the endless dark
as you slide and scramble down
into that pit by the highway subconscious,
looking for those needles and pins in the dirt
    and the dark, begging for pain, fingers
scrounging dry rock until they bleed, and in the most
desperate epoch your fingers clutch
what you once cast away
with such hate—a relief, your heart;

// but //

no desert can evade the rains forever; you will hardscrabble
down that same darkness one day, one future;
torrential comeuppance and floodtide prayers, for
all that is found will be lost again
    and again
in the blighted ravines of that midnight memory

Recriminations

the television stares blank and gray
into the empty room where your parents
once sat and repeated a call for civility
and decency as they knitted socks to the tune
of men laughing on the screen about children
in cages and dead Mexicans in cargo holds
baking in the sun, with more to come
after the next commercial break;

unless you turn it off and let the gray silence
say all there is to say about this world we made
and lost

Parables

the way it was, you see,
isn't the way it was

parables of sunny mornings
in small towns with steeples,
8 a.m. mill factory whistles,
the Cleavers and the Huxtables
waving hello as paychecks are
cashed into a whole string of
holidays and new cars and all
those stories of yesteryear are
like so much morning mist,
burned away to the shocking truth
by the searing clarity of the sun

everyone has stories they tell
themselves to absolve the pain
of their willfully ignorant lives

however,

this story sees you as a spec of light
in a universe tumbling toward chaos,
bones on fire on a carousel before
anyone got to say goodbye to anyone,
and the question you need to ask is,
is this just a story your heart tells?
or is this your truth lying in wait?

you are aware the past isn't as it was
and you long to make things right

but the world moves so fast and leaves
you so far behind that you grab on to
any buoy, lifeline, lit torch, flag, or
bottle of snake oil to guide you along
the pathway into the dark future ahead
(but again, this is a myth and a fable)
(you are cosmic and nothing) (part of
everything at once, the endless well of
energy and being/non-being) and you
walk forward with the crowd (which
exists in this particular consciousness)
feeling out the new universe you intend
to build in mirror image of the past you
crave, trying to stave away the horrors
coming in over the radio, reports of boots
crushing the skulls of children, rivers on
fire, hospitals full of the dead and dying,
the last dolphin harpooned for pleasure
—and it works, it works, you are glowing
with the fire of the movement, of willful
ignorance that your years of inaction have
no consequences at all, that your endeavors
to create a better economic pleasure cruise
have finally helped you stave away the evils
THEY sought to reap in this crisp clean world
of yours, and oh, now you remember why love
and freedom exist at all, as the great tidal wave
of fire you worked so hard to ignore lo these
many years rips through the carousel of your
life—and just like that

you're gone

Bereave

one shoe on as the afternoon sun forms mathematics across
the wall in white and gray, begins to hedge away vision and
time, rushing through morning streets to one funeral home,
then the next, an uncle, a grandfather, a friend, rain and
death one after another so that the black suit begins to feel
like skin, begins to box you in like a coffin, soft silk and a
pillow, accelerating through a red light // park and breathe,
the line of those paying respects waits within, and down the
street another, and up the highway a hole in the damp earth
to be filled and forgotten, like a tree in a forest you cannot
see for the fog, a traffic light, another yellow turning red and
a parking lot, the watch on your wrist has stopped and you
feel you will never be able to close the car door, walk the black
macadam to a room where now you stand among many, but
one day // one day you'll lie in wait, already gone, a sapling
on the shore of some distant land of sun and silence

Acre

a parcel of geography held dear, where as a child on late
night drives home from supermarkets or grandparents you
wake in a half daze and feel the mental constrictions coiling
around your heart, imagining the car flying off the road into
this lake, through that field, tires catching the shoulder rut
and yawning into a ravine, rolling out of control past your
driveway down the lawn into the back acre where a soggy
creek sucks down the car's weight, yet somehow you always
make it home fine, your parents and loved ones safe, though
the fear always seeps into that half-conscious state as you
race through the dark for that tract of home and hearth in
the middle of nowhere, and the total loss of control will
only come later, not in a car but in a body running rampant
through that long night of life toward a plot of land all your
own, a soft earthly embrace holding you dear among the
pines and headstones reaching for a moon that doesn't even
know they exist

Stage Right

it's true that we extricate ourselves from meaning and geography but no matter how many umbilical cords we sever in our many tumultuous departures, there are shadows that never leave the walls and memories that repeat themselves upon the consciousness of those we've passed through in our fading, fading timelines—do not think they don't still damage, or sooth, or reprimand in voices not unlike cicadas in high summer, soft and shrill in the back fields of our existence; they remain, they sing out, hoping to find you again when the world finally blinks and these corporeal theatrics cease to appear, and slip into the folds of the ethereal like a player exiting stage right only to whisper and wait for their next line

Dandelions in the Dark

the small dry length of pavement you found
  after walking from the bus station to the bar
where you said you'd meet them for a bloody
  mary the next morning, but the bus arrived so
late the hotels were all full and you felt so sick
  and lonely and tired from the 10 hour bus ride up
the spine of California with two long breakdowns
  along the side of the highway, one misery after another,
and so you walked around to the back alley and
  slipped down out of sight, on the ground, and even
in the dark of night you saw dandelions sprouting up
  through San Francisco pavement cracks and you
somehow knew you'd make it through even if
  it all led to nothing spectacular, simply being alive
would be victory enough, though you also knew
  death wasn't a failure but an inevitability,
like the stars just visible in the orange glowing
  sky overhead, making it through the long vast
darkness to die in your eyes, a miracle,
  and you thought how the pavement wasn't so
bad after all—sleep came, dawn came, and
  one day death and a bloody mary would too
while the world and stars and San Francisco
  kept spinning into the maw forever

Fedora

window arteries of black rain stream through red apoplectic
lights of neon and bitter halogen where the moonlight dies
reaching for empty holsters, guns gone, carried away by the
hands of the clock, hour of agony in this office overlooking
34th Street, rain and chaos, knots of taxis, umbrellas like
beetles scurry to subway stairs down into the darkness, but
up here there is only death and dust, each a stabbing accusa-
tion telling me there is a grinning devil somewhere out there
crushing a headstone with delight; he waits with a gasoline
smile, you wait with an empty whisky bottle, a hand without
a gun, white bones burdened by shame, craving time to make
this last crime correct, but all the time you already wasted
in this life is just an unsigned confession they'll lay on your
chest before they close the casket, a sentence six feet deep
where you'll have to make due with unfinished business, a
silken kiss in the dark, but never the red curtain falling to
applause, your heart forever one beat shy of love

Tao of the City

bottle shard sidewalks
and the deadly peacefulness
of footsteps cutting through red
and green lights glowing
overhead at night, no
cars at all 'cept for a yellow
taxi parked, the cabbie
taking a look at me and quickly turning
away, back to the late
night radio program on the edge
of midnight—
they're talking about cops killing
and cops dying and the heat
keeps beating down from above
and the ground drying up
from below and I wonder who
is not sleepless now
here in humanity's catacomb?

the mornings rush with fuel and gold,
but at night, nothing grows in this place,
not madness, not hope, not any weeping crop,
not here in the shadows of dead museums
or at the feet of sleeping hotel doormen
dreaming of cities full of churches
and no pews to fill them, standing room
services, praying like drunks for
one more drop, for sheets of rain against
their doormen dreaming hats

and then they wake to the
pall of reality, the constant death toll
rising, but the only number that
matters is *none*, no more killing and
no more killed, and the cabbie
is wise to look away, because
no matter how much you want to believe
nobody knows anyone's mind anymore
as the echoes of midnight feet
dance through bottle shard
streets, a sort of Tao of the city
balancing fear and love
on the broken edge of filthy faith

Orchid

she drinks wine in her hotel room
a dying orchid on fire
watching the bottles go down
one / by / one

wavering along with one hand
on the wall down
the long alley of life—
there are doors shut to us all,
hewing a singular path scarred by
lamppost lights razing the night

that final alley leads to the end
where the rain machine rakes across
the skin of the flat dark sea—
she will dive the depths,
down into the grip and the swell
letting go of shoes and sense,
waterlogged cigarettes,
pictures slipping from the heart

/ the darkness within the dark /

looking up one might see
the rippled skin of the sea,
the wavering lamppost lights,
rain on the window of an empty hotel,
bed unmade,
wine dried to dust,

her ghosts only now coming to life

eager to bloom like smoke
from a candle
blown out too soon

Great Plains and Galaxies Beyond

her favorite bartender told me she disappeared two years ago, followed some guy to Kansas to chase aliens or tornadoes or both, left her corner stool and took all her pain and memories and Hollywood trinkets with her, and all down the boulevard in Montrose the homeless walk the sun-washed streets like anyone else, afraid of the local cops, afraid of the night and who might take what little else they have, but one town over they still ticket a man who sets up a food truck in the town square after dusk to give out free dinners to anyone, ticketed again and again by cops who can't even look the man in the eye, won't even acknowledge the homeless wandering off to eat and sleep and dream like anyone else does as halogen and neon takes hold of the night, satellites and spaceships overhead, souls lost and spun out across the Great Plains and galaxies beyond searching for answers, for meaning, for some reason to keep moving forward, all too often never finding what they're looking for, but maybe, just maybe…

Demarcation

the last thing inscribed
was "her eyes swing away
like blue jays in flight"
but it was the old notebook
and I couldn't remember
who it was about—maybe
nobody I knew

so, a stranger then,
a woman with blue eyes
who departed a train along
the Hudson River some years
back whose eyes sail
like birds in flight

into another lifespan

and then,
in the old notebook,
a black line beneath demarcating
the years passing by

followed by nothing at all

Intimations

in the dark of our room your lips seem to move but I have
long ago lost my sense of hearing and all I can hold on to are
the dreams that come to me wrapped in pink sheets, memory
foam, your soft skin along the curve of your shoulder where
I close my eyes and burrow, envisioning your lips and all the
intimations they may hold in the night

Intercontinental

the sun sets and keeps setting, a tidal wave of night cross-
ing the globe, bringing love and drunken revelry, bringing
exhaustion and loneliness to small rented rooms, bringing
light pollution to endless downtowns, bringing 10,000
people to a row of benches in an airport terminal, a jet
stream of strangers using the same space to rest, to regroup,
to move forward, onto impossible contraptions carrying
us to islands, to mountains, to desert airstrips or midnight
fields in Europe where snowflakes fall in graceful pirouettes
as the sun sets halfway across the globe on a stranger's antic-
ipation for the night and all it might bring with its tidal wave
embrace

Grunewald

along cobbled Berlin streets the trees all have numbers nailed to them on little wooden placards and the doors too, I follow them along quiet sidewalks edged with November snow peppered with soot and wet cigarettes // after a long flight and endless nights fighting the six-hour time difference there is a revelation: peace in the cemetery nearby, benches and tall hedgerows quiet, trees twisted like Van Gogh paintings towering into the gray morning sky domed over ancient Berlin and ghosts beside me, wavering over cobble, along the headstones, the cold November bench of marble // years later I sometimes think I'll wake and find myself there, across the many lifetimes and ocean swells, the deep cold Atlantic, the farms dotting Lorraine-Alsace, all the way to those headstones in a row, ghosts and vines crawling, searching, dying, reborn // I live winter, I dream spring, I ache summer, I rise come autumn and at night I walk the hedgerows eternal staring into falling white snow frosting the edges of brown yellow leaves, waiting for the pages to run out and all the clocks in the world to pause and point to the penultimate end all be all we all dream about but only meet once in a lifetime, and then \\\

Publication Notes

"Umbra" appeared in *Pine Hills Review*

"Fedora" appeared in Dumpster Fire Press

"Downtown" appeared in *Book of Matches*

"Affliction" appeared in *Live Nude Poems*

"Grunewald" appeared in *The Westchester Review*

"Fugue" appeared in *The Mantle*

"Marathon" and "Dandelions in the Dark" appeared in *San Pedro River Review*

"An Unordered List of Things That Remain" appeared in *Trailer Park Quarterly*

A version of "Orchid" appeared in *The Gasconade Review*

"Pioneer" appeared in *Trampoline Magazine*

"Acre" appeared in *Tabula Rasa Review*

"Pastoral" won honorable mention in the Stephen A. DiBiase Poetry Prize

James H. Duncan is the editor of *Hobo Camp Review*, a former editor at *Writer's Digest*, and the author of *Proper Etiquette in the Slaughterhouse Line*, *Both Ways Home*, *We Are All Terminal But This Exit Is Mine*, *Vacancy*, *Nights Without Rain*, and *Tributaries*, among other books of poetry and fiction. He resides in upstate New York but travels widely to review indie bookstores for his blog, The Bookshop Hunter. For more of his poetry and essays, visit www.jameshduncan.com.

MORE ROADSIDE PRESS TITLES:

By Plane, Train or Coincidence
Michele McDannold

Prying
Jack Micheline, Charles Bukowski and Catfish McDaris

Wolf Whistles Behind the Dumpster
Dan Provost

*Busking Blues: Recollections of a Chicago Street Musician
and Squatter*
Westley Heine

Unknowable Things
Kerry Trautman

How to Play House
Heather Dorn

Kiss the Heathens
Ryan Quinn Flanagan

St. James Infirmary
Steven Meloan

Street Corner Spirits
Westley Heine

A Room Above a Convenience Store
William Taylor Jr.

Resurrection Song
George Wallace

Nothing and Too Much to Talk About
Nancy Patrice Davenport

Bar Guide for the Seriously Deranged
Alan Catlin

MORE ROADSIDE PRESS TITLES:

Born on Good Friday
Nathan Graziano

Under Normal Conditions
Karl Koweski

The Dead and the Desperate
Dan Denton

Clown Gravy
Misti Rainwater-Lites

Walking Away
Michael D. Grover

All in a Pretty Little Row
Dan Provost

These Are the People in Your Neighbourhood
Jordan Trethewey

They Said I Wasn't College Material
Scot Young

Radio Water
Francine Witte

And Blackberries Grew Wild
Susan Mickelberry

Licorice Heart
Miles Budimir

Disposable Darlings
Todd Cirillo

Full Moon Midnight
Belinda Subraman

Innocent Postcards
John Pietaro